# RIBBON STAR QUILTS

### Nancy Mahoney

Martingale®
& COMPANY

## ACKNOWLEDGMENTS

It takes a team of hardworking and talented people to create a quilt book. I wish to thank the enthusiastic people at Martingale & Company, for without your many talents there would be no book!

A huge thank-you and a big hug to Dawn Kelly, machine quilter extraordinaire; her imagination and talent add the extra dimension that brings the quilts to life.

Special thanks to the following companies who generously provided so many great products: P & B Textiles, whose marvelous fabrics created "Mosaic Stars," "Jungle Stars," and "Polka-Dot Stars"; Northcott/ Monarch, whose lovely fabrics created "Garden Stars"; American & Efird and Marci Brier for Mettler and Signature threads; and Hobbs Bonded Fibers and H.D. Wilbanks for batting.

And thanks most of all to Tom Reichert, whose constant help, support, and understanding makes everything possible.

Ribbon Star Quilts
© 2008 by Nancy Mahoney

That Patchwork Place® is an imprint of Martingale & Company®.

Martingale & Company
20205 144th Ave. NE
Woodinville, WA 98072-8478 USA
www.martingale-pub.com

## CREDITS

| | |
|---|---|
| President & CEO | Tom Wierzbicki |
| Publisher | Jane Hamada |
| Editorial Director | Mary V. Green |
| Managing Editor | Tina Cook |
| Developmental Editor | Karen Costello Soltys |
| Technical Editor | Cyndi Hershey |
| Copy Editor | Liz McGehee |
| Design Director | Stan Green |
| Assistant Design Director | Regina Girard |
| Illustrator | Laurel Strand |
| Cover & Text Designer | Stan Green |
| Photographer | Brent Kane |

Printed in China
13 12 11 10 09 08      8 7 6 5 4 3 2 1

**Library of Congress Cataloging-in-Publication Data**
Library of Congress Control Number: 2007034052

ISBN: 978-1-56477-793-5

## MISSION STATEMENT

Dedicated to providing quality products and service to inspire creativity.

# CONTENTS

# Introduction

*One day I was working on my computer, drawing blocks and creating quilts for my book* Square Deal *(Martingale & Company, 2007) when I came up with a block I later named "Strip Star." I continued to play with the Strip Star block to see how many variations of the same basic block I could create. But when I set the blocks side by side, I realized it looked as though a ribbon was woven between the stars. And in a short time, the idea for a Ribbon Star Quilts book had sprung to life.*

On the pages that follow, you will find five quilts, each with its own distinctive look even though they are all made from the same basic block. In the "Making the Blocks" section on pages 7–9, I will show you how to make the basic block by cutting rectangle units from strip sets and sewing the units together with a partial seam.

When you look at the quilts, you'll see there are several elements that make each quilt special, the first being the fabric. I like to start with my outer-border fabric and select other fabrics to complement it. Notice also how the number of strips and the width of the strips used to create the rectangle units are different in each quilt. I discovered how making these small changes produces an array of exciting possibilities.

I hope these quilts spark your creativity and that you enjoy making them as much as I did. I encourage you to make these quilts your own. Quilting is a wonderful creative outlet and is a joy to share with everyone.

—Nancy

# MAKING THE BLOCKS

*On the following pages, you will find valuable information for the successful completion of your quilt. All of the specific techniques needed to create your Ribbon Star quilt blocks are covered in this section.*

## Quiltmaking Basics

The projects in this book use basic cutting and piecing techniques that are familiar to most quilters.

### TOOLS

Basic rotary-cutting tools include a rotary cutter, an 18" x 24" cutting mat, and a 6" x 24" acrylic ruler. For the projects in this book, I also recommend an 8½"-square ruler for cutting the rectangle units. Note that rotary-cutting instructions are written for right-handers; reverse the instructions if you are left-handed.

### Cutting Bias Strips

To make the rectangle units for the blocks in each quilt project, you will need to cut bias strips in various widths. Why bias strips? All of the strips are positioned at a 45° angle within each of the rectangular units. Since strip sets are used to create these units, each individual strip must be cut at a 45° angle (bias). This maintains the straight of grain on the outer edges of the units, keeping the units stable.

The fabric for these strips will first be cut into 18"-wide strips across the width of the fabric. These 18" x 42" rectangles make the strip-cutting process much easier. To cut the bias strips, lay the fabric rectangle flat with right side facing up. Note that it's very important that the fabric is always placed right side up. Align the 45° line on your rotary-cutting ruler with a selvage edge of the fabric. Cut along the ruler edge and trim off the corner. If your ruler is not long enough to complete the cut, you will need to slide your ruler down just a bit and cut again to finish.

Carefully cut the bias strips in the required width for the quilt you are making. To cut strips, use the edge of the first cut as a guide, and align the desired strip-width measurement on the ruler with the cut edge of the fabric. Continue to cut strips across the fabric until you have the number specified. You'll have a large triangle left over at the beginning and end of each piece. Save these for another project.

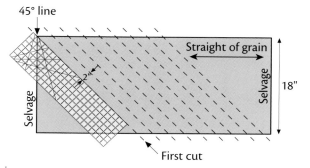

### STARCHED FABRICS

If you have prewashed your fabric, you may find that starching it before cutting will replace the body and make it more cooperative when you cut bias strips. You can starch your fabric by first covering your ironing board with a large towel. Spray starch on the back of dry fabric until it is truly wet. Let the starch soak in a bit and then iron until the fabric is dry. Fabric that has not been prewashed has a crisper feel and usually doesn't need to be starched.

## Making Strip Sets and Block Units

For each quilt project, you'll start by cutting the specified fabrics into 18" x 42" pieces. By cutting the pieces this way, they will be easier to handle and will fit on your rotary-cutting mat. If you have two or more 18" pieces from one fabric, you may want to layer the pieces so that they can all be cut at the same time. To do this, after pressing all of the pieces, lay the first piece with right side up. Then, place the second piece, right side up, on top of the first piece, aligning one selvage edge and one cut edge. Repeat to layer additional pieces.

1. Referring to "Cutting Bias Strips" on page 7, cut the exact number of strips in the various widths specified for the quilt you are making. Arrange the strips in the correct order as shown in the quilt-project illustration.

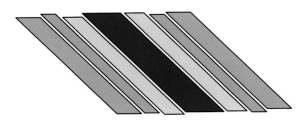

2. With right sides together; sew the strips together along the long bias edges, offsetting the point at the top edge ¼" as shown. Be sure to align the ends of the strips so that one edge forms as straight a line as possible. Sew all of the strips together to make a strip set and then press the seam allowances in one direction. The number of strip sets you need to make is specified in the quilt-project instructions.

Offset strips ¼".

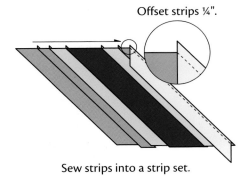

Sew strips into a strip set.

3. Beginning at the lower-left section and using an 8½" square ruler, position the ruler on a strip set so that the corner of the ruler is on one seam line and the 5½" mark is on the opposite seam line of the same strip as shown. *Note that the ruler will always be positioned on the strip that measures a 2⅛" finished width (2⅝" cut). I think of this strip as the "ribbon" strip.*

4. Each rectangle unit will require four cuts. The first and second cuts are along the right side and top edge of the ruler. These cuts remove the "oversized" rectangle from the strip set.

Ribbon strip

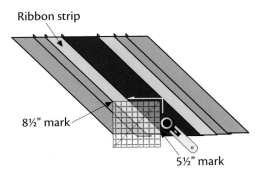

8½" mark

5½" mark

5. The third and fourth cuts are along the remaining two sides. They trim the rectangle unit to the correct size, 5½" x 8½", which includes seam allowance. To make the cuts, turn the segment from step 4 and align the 5½" and 8½" measurements on the ruler with the two cut edges as shown. Cut the remaining two sides of the rectangle unit.

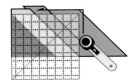

Turn cut segment
and cut opposite 2 sides.

### SEAM CONTROL
As you cut the rectangle units, separate them into two mirror image stacks. Have the large triangle face right in one stack and left in the other, as shown in step 1 of "Making the Blocks" on page 12. Taking a little time now to organize the units will save you time when sewing the units into blocks and again when sewing the blocks together.

## MAKING A MASKING-TAPE GUIDE

I like using an 8½" square ruler because I only have to remember the 5½" mark when positioning the ruler on the strip set. If you do not have an 8½" square ruler, you can use a ruler that's a different size, as long as it's larger than 5½" x 8½". When using a different-size ruler, it's helpful to place masking tape along the appropriate markings. If you are using an 8½" square ruler, you may want to place masking tape along the 5½" line.

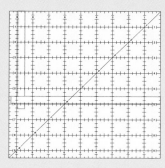

Marking tape used to indicate
5½" x 8½" area

6. Continue cutting rectangle units from each strip set in this manner, working from left to right and from bottom to top, until you have cut units from all usable fabric and have the number of units specified for each quilt project. Each strip set will yield six 5½" x 8½" rectangles.

## Assembling the Blocks

The blocks are stitched using a partial-seam technique, which looks tricky but it's not!

1. Arrange four rectangle units and one center square according to the block illustrations in each quilt project.

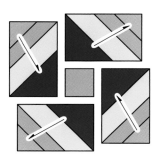

2. Sew one rectangle unit to the center square, leaving about 1" open at the end of the square. Press all seam allowances toward the center square.

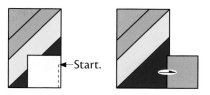

←Start.

3. Sew a rectangle unit to the unit from step 2 as shown; press.

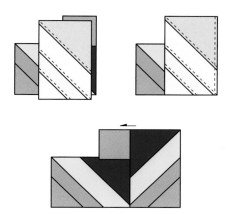

4. Sew the third rectangle unit to the unit from step 3; press. Sew the final rectangle unit to the block; press. Sew the small open section of the center-square seam closed to complete the block; press.

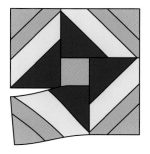
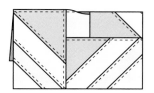

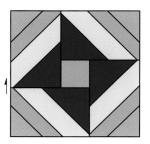

# MOSAIC STARS

*This quilt is the simplest in this book because you need only four fabrics for the strip sets plus one additional fabric for the block center. Be sure to look at the alternate version on page 13.*

**Finished Quilt Size:** 68½" x 81½"
**Finished Block Size:** 13" x 13"

## Materials

*Yardage is based on 42"-wide fabric.*

4⅞ yards of large-scale purple floral print for blocks, outer border, and binding

3¾ yards of small-scale purple floral print for blocks and inner border

3½ yards of yellow print for blocks and middle border

2¼ yards of green print for blocks

¼ yard of dark purple print for block centers

5¼ yards of fabric for backing (2 widths pieced vertically)

73" x 86" piece of batting

| CUTTING | | | | |
|---------|-----|---------------|-------------|-------------|
| **Fabric** | **Use** | **Number to Cut** | **Size to Cut** | **Bias Strips\*** |
| Large-scale purple print | Blocks | 5 pieces | 18" x 42" | 14 strips, 5" wide |
| Large-scale purple print | Outer border | 4 lengthwise strips | 6¼" x 72" | — |
| Large-scale purple print | Binding | 5 lengthwise strips | 2" x 63" | — |
| Yellow print | Blocks | 6 pieces | 18" x 42" | 28 strips, 2⅝" wide |
| Yellow print | Middle border | 7 strips | 1¼" x 42" | — |
| Green print | Blocks | 4 pieces | 18" x 42" | 28 strips, 2" wide |
| Small-scale purple print | Blocks | 6 pieces | 18" x 42" | 28 strips, 3" wide |
| Small-scale purple print | Inner border | 7 strips | 2" x 42" | — |
| Dark purple print | Block centers | 20 squares | 3½" x 3½" | — |

*Refer to "Cutting Bias Strips" on page 7 for detailed instructions if needed.

## Making the Blocks

1. Refer to "Making Strip Sets and Block Units" on page 7 to arrange and sew the strips together as shown. Press the seam allowances in one direction. Make 14 strip sets. Cut *each* strip set into six 5½" x 8½" rectangle units for a total of 84 units. You will have four extra rectangles.

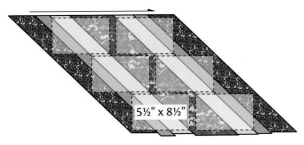

5½" x 8½"

Make 14 strip sets.
Cut 6 units from each strip set (84 total).

2. For ease in sewing the units together, arrange four rectangle units from step 1 as shown. Place the units so that the top-right and bottom-left units have the seam allowances pressed toward the outside edges. The top-left and bottom-right units should have the seam allowances pressed toward the center. Referring to "Assembling the Blocks" on page 9, sew the units and a dark purple 3½" square together using a partial seam technique. Make 20 blocks.

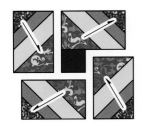 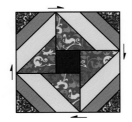

Make 20.

## Assembling the Quilt Top

1. Arrange the blocks into five horizontal rows with four blocks each as shown in the assembly diagram.

2. Sew the blocks into rows. Press the seams in alternate directions from row to row. Stitch the rows together. Press the seams in one direction.

3. Sew the small-scale purple print 2" x 42" strips together end to end. Press seams open. Measure the length of the quilt through the center. From the pieced strip, cut two strips to this size. Sew one strip to each side of the quilt. Press seams toward the border.

4. Measure the width of the quilt through the center, including the side borders. Use the remaining pieced strip to cut two strips to this size and sew to the top and bottom of the quilt; press.

5. Repeat steps 3 and 4 using the yellow 1¼" x 42" strips.

6. Measure the quilt as described in steps 3 and 4 to cut and sew outer-border strips using the purple 6¼" x 72" strips; press. Because these strips are cut on the lengthwise grain, they do not need to be pieced together before cutting the borders.

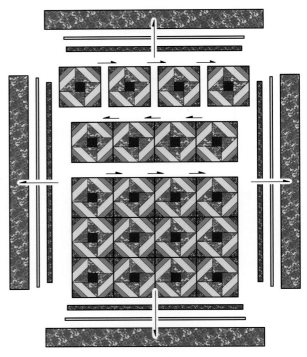

Assembly diagram

## Finishing the Quilt

1. Layer the quilt with batting and the pieced backing; baste. Hand or machine quilt as desired or refer to the quilting diagram that shows how the sample quilt was quilted.

2. Trim the batting and backing so the edges are even with the quilt top. Use the large-scale purple print 2" x 63" strips to bind the quilt.

## QUILTING SUGGESTION

### POLKA-DOT STARS

I thought you might enjoy seeing a wall hanging with dramatic colors and whimsical dots—a real change from the sophisticated floral prints in the "Mosaic Stars" quilt. I'm always surprised at how the choice of fabric, color, and value placement can change the personality of a quilt design. For this version, I also made a slight change to the block. I arranged the rectangle units so that the largest triangle was on the outside edges of the block instead of in the center.

**Finished Size:** 53½" x 53½"

# GARDEN STARS

*This wonderful quilt is created using five different strip widths. I also used different fabrics in opposite corners of the block to add variety.*

**Finished Quilt Size:** 50" x 63"
**Finished Block Size:** 13" x 13"

## Materials

*Yardage is based on 42"-wide fabric.*

2⅞ yards of mint-and-pink floral print for blocks and outer border

2¼ yards of light pink tonal print for blocks

2 yards of dark pink tonal print for blocks, inner border, and binding

1⅔ yards of pink-on-white print for blocks

1⅛ yards of medium pink print for blocks

1⅛ yards of small-scale pink floral print for blocks

3⅜ yards of fabric for backing (2 widths pieced horizontally)

54" x 67" piece of batting

| CUTTING | | | | |
|---|---|---|---|---|
| **Fabric** | **Use** | **Number to Cut** | **Size to Cut** | **Bias Strips*** |
| Mint-and-pink floral print | Blocks | 2 pieces | 18" x 42" | 8 strips, 3¾" wide |
| Mint-and-pink floral print | Outer border | 4 lengthwise strips | 5" x 56" | — |
| Dark pink tonal print | Blocks | 2 pieces | 18" x 42" | 16 strips, 1½" wide |
| Dark pink tonal print | Binding | 6 strips | 2" x 42" | — |
| Dark pink tonal print | Inner border | 5 strips | 1¼" x 42" | — |
| Dark pink tonal print | Block centers | 12 squares | 3½" x 3½" | — |
| Light pink tonal print | Blocks | 4 pieces | 18" x 42" | 16 strips, 2⅝" wide |
| Pink-on-white print | Blocks | 3 pieces | 18" x 42" | 16 strips, 2" wide |
| Medium pink print | Blocks | 2 pieces | 18" x 42" | 8 strips, 3" wide |
| Small-scale pink floral print | Blocks | 2 pieces | 18" x 42" | 8 strips, 3" wide |

*Refer to "Cutting Bias Strips" on page 7 for detailed instructions if needed.

## MAKING THE BLOCKS

1. Refer to "Making Strip Sets and Block Units" on page 7 to arrange and sew the strips together as shown. Press the seam allowances in one direction. Make eight strip sets. Cut *each* strip set into six 5½" x 8½" rectangle units for a total of 48 units.

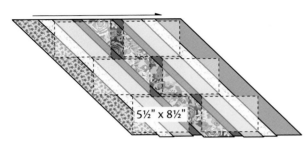

Make 8 strip sets.
Cut 6 units from each strip set (48 total).

2. For ease in sewing the units together, arrange four rectangle units from step 1 as shown. Position the units so that the top-right and bottom-left units have the seam allowances pressed toward the outside edges. The top-left and bottom-right units will have the seam allowances pressed toward the center. Referring to "Assembling the Blocks" on page 9, sew the units and a dark pink 3½" square together using a partial seam technique. Make 12 blocks.

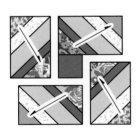 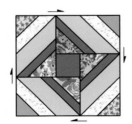

Make 12.

## ASSEMBLING THE QUILT TOP

1. Arrange the blocks into four horizontal rows of three blocks each as shown in the assembly diagram.

2. Sew the blocks into rows. Press the seams in alternate directions from row to row. Stitch the rows together. Press the seams in one direction.

3. Sew the dark pink 1¼" x 42" strips together end to end. Press seams open. Measure the length of the quilt through the center. From the pieced strip, cut

two strips to this size. Sew one strip to each side of the quilt. Press seams toward the border.

4. Measure the width of the quilt through the center, including the side borders. Use the remaining pieced strip to cut two strips to this size and sew them to the top and bottom of the quilt; press.

5. Measure the quilt as described in steps 3 and 4 to cut and sew outer-border strips using the mint-and-pink 5" x 56" strips; press. Because these strips are cut on the lengthwise grain, they do not need to be pieced together.

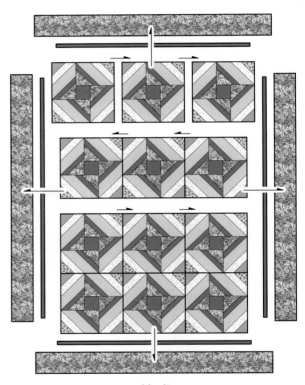

Assembly diagram

## FINISHING THE QUILT

1. Layer the quilt with batting and the pieced backing; baste. Hand or machine quilt as desired or refer to the quilting diagram that shows how the sample quilt was quilted.

2. Trim the batting and backing so the edges are even with the quilt top. Use the dark pink 2" x 42" strips to bind the quilt.

## QUILTING SUGGESTION

**Finished Size: 49" x 23"**

### SUNFLOWER STARS TABLE RUNNER

This table runner features dark navy stars and a perky sunflower print border. It looks nothing like the soft, romantic floral design of the "Garden Stars" quilt. This table runner needs only three blocks and simple borders and could easily be completed in one day.

# CHRISTMAS STARS

*F*or this quilt, I combined the four-strip block from "Mosaic Stars" on page 10 and the five-strip block from "Garden Stars" on page 14. Use the traditional red and green color scheme as I did and you'll be instantly ready for the Christmas season.

**Finished Quilt Size:** 82" x 95"
**Finished Block Size:** 13" x 13"

## Materials

*Yardage is based on 42"-wide fabric.*

4¾ yards of red-and-green leaves print for blocks and outer border

4½ yards of dark green tonal print for blocks

2¼ yards of red print 1 for blocks and binding

2¼ yards of red print 3 for blocks

2¼ yards of cream print for blocks

1⅔ yards of light green print for blocks

1⅔ yards of red print 2 for blocks

1⅔ yards of yellow tonal print for blocks

⅞ yard of red print 4 for block centers and inner border

8 yards of fabric for backing (3 widths pieced horizontally)

87" x 100" piece of batting

| CUTTING | | | | |
|---|---|---|---|---|
| **Fabric** | **Use** | **Number to Cut** | **Size to Cut** | **Bias Strips*** |
| Red-and-green leaves print | Blocks | 4 pieces | 18" x 42" | 10 strips, 5" wide |
| Red-and-green leaves print | Outer border | 4 lengthwise strips | 7½" x 84" | — |
| Dark green print | Blocks | 8 pieces | 18" x 42" | 40 strips, 2⅝" wide |
| Red print 1 | Blocks | 3 pieces | 18" x 42" | 20 strips, 1⅞" wide |
| Red print 1 | Binding | 10 strips | 2" x 42" | — |
| Cream print | Blocks | 4 pieces | 18" x 42" | 20 strips, 3" wide |
| Yellow print | Blocks | 3 pieces | 18" x 42" | 10 strips, 3¼" wide |
| Red print 2 | Blocks | 3 pieces | 18" x 42" | 20 strips, 1⅞" wide |
| Light green print | Blocks | 3 pieces | 18" x 42" | 20 strips, 1⅞" wide |
| Red print 3 | Blocks | 4 pieces | 18" x 42" | 20 strips, 3" wide |
| Red print 4 | Block centers | 30 squares | 3½" x 3½" | — |
| Red print 4 | Inner border | 8 strips | 1¾" x 42" | — |

*Refer to "Cutting Bias Strips" on page 7 for detailed instructions if needed.

## Making the Blocks

1. Refer to "Making Strip Sets and Block Units" on page 7 to arrange and sew the strips together as shown. Press the seam allowances in one direction. Make 10 strip sets from *each* combination of fabrics, 20 total. Cut *each* strip set into six 5½" x 8½" rectangle units for a total of 60 units for strip set A and 60 units for strip set B. Keep the units from each combination of fabrics together.

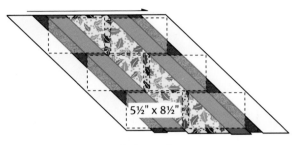

Strip set A.
Make 10. Cut 6 units from
each strip set (60 total).

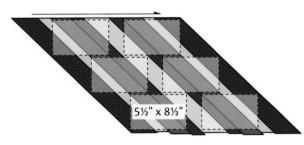

Strip set B.
Make 10. Cut 6 units from
each strip set (60 total).

2. For ease in sewing the units together, arrange four rectangle units from strip set A as shown above right. The top-right and bottom-left units will have the seam allowances pressed toward the outside edges. The top-left and bottom-right units will have the seam allowances pressed toward the center. Refer to "Assembling the Blocks" on page 9 to sew the units

and a red 3½" square together using the partial seam technique. Make 15 blocks and label as block A. Using four rectangle units from strip set B and a red square, repeat to make 15 blocks and label as block B.

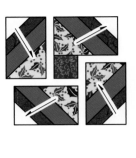 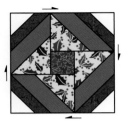

Block A.
Make 15.

 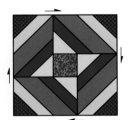

Block B.
Make 15.

## Assembling the Quilt Top

1. Referring to the diagram on the facing page, arrange the blocks in six horizontal rows of five blocks each, alternating block A and block B in each row and from row to row.

2. Sew the blocks into rows. Press the seams in alternate directions from row to row. Stitch the rows together. Press the seams in one direction.

3. Sew the red 1¾" x 42" strips together end to end. Press seams open. Measure the length of the quilt through the center. From the pieced strip, cut two strips to this size. Sew one strip to each side of the quilt. Press seams toward the border.

4. Measure the width of the quilt through the center, including the side borders. Use the remaining pieced strip to cut two strips to this size and sew to the top and bottom of the quilt; press.

**5.** Measure the quilt as described in steps 3 and 4 to cut and sew outer-border strips using the red-and-green 7½" x 84" strips; press. Because these strips are cut on the lengthwise grain, they do not need to be pieced together.

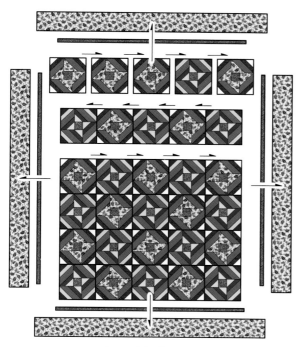

Assembly diagram

## FINISHING THE QUILT

**1.** Layer the quilt with batting and the pieced backing; baste. Hand or machine quilt as desired or refer to the quilting diagram that shows how the sample quilt was quilted.

**2.** Trim the batting and backing so the edges are even with the quilt top. Use the red 2" x 42" strips to bind the quilt.

### QUILTING SUGGESTION

# STARS AND STRIPES

*B*elieve it or not, this is also a five-strip block like the one used in "Garden Stars" on page 14.

I just changed the width of the strips and used two colors to create the ribbon. The red-

white-and-blue color scheme gets you ready to celebrate all of those patriotic holidays!

**Finished Quilt Size:** 65½" x 65½"
**Finished Block Size:** 13" x 13"

## Materials

*Yardage is based on 42"-wide fabric.*

3⅝ yards of red-and-blue print for blocks and outer border

1⅔ yards of cream print 1 for blocks

1⅔ yards of light blue print 1 for blocks

1⅔ yards of light blue print 2 for blocks

1⅔ yards of dark blue print for blocks

1⅔ yards of red print for blocks

1⅛ yards of cream print 2 for blocks

1 yard of blue stripe for block centers, inner border, and binding

4⅜ yards of fabric for backing

70" x 70" piece of batting

| CUTTING | | | | |
|---|---|---|---|---|
| **Fabric** | **Use** | **Number to Cut** | **Size to Cut** | **Bias Strips*** |
| Red-and-blue print | Blocks | 3 pieces | 18" x 42" | 11 strips, 3¾" wide |
| Red-and-blue print | Outer border | 4 lengthwise strips | 6" x 68" | — |
| Cream print 1 | Blocks | 3 pieces | 18" x 42" | 22 strips, 1½" wide |
| Light blue print 1 | Blocks | 3 pieces | 18" x 42" | 11 strips, 2⅝" wide |
| Dark blue print | Blocks | 3 pieces | 18" x 42" | 11 strips, 2⅝" wide |
| Cream print 2 | Blocks | 2 pieces | 18" x 42" | 22 strips, 1¼" wide |
| Light blue print 2 | Blocks | 3 pieces | 18" x 42" | 11 strips, 3¾" wide |
| Red print | Blocks | 3 pieces | 18" x 42" | 11 strips, 3¾" wide |
| Blue stripe | Block centers | 16 squares | 3½" x 3½" | — |
| Blue stripe | Inner border | 6 strips | 1½" x 42" | — |
| Blue stripe | Binding | 7 strips | 2" x 42" | — |
| *Refer to "Cutting Bias Strips" on page 7 for detailed instructions if needed.* | | | | |

## MAKING THE BLOCKS

1. Refer to "Making Strip Sets and Block Units" on page 7 to arrange and sew the strips together as shown. Press the seam allowances in one direction. Make 11 strip sets. Cut *each* strip set into six 5½" x 8½" rectangle units for a total of 66 units. You will have two extra rectangles.

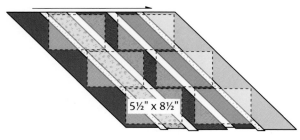

Make 11 strip sets.
Cut 6 units from each strip set (66 total).

2. For ease in sewing the units together, arrange four rectangle units as shown. The top-right and bottom-left units will have the seam allowances pressed toward the outside edges. The top-left and bottom-right units will have the seam allowances pressed toward the center. Refer to "Assembling the Blocks" on page 9 to sew the units and a blue stripe 3½" square together using the partial seam technique. Make 16 blocks.

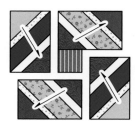 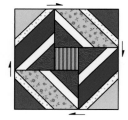

Make 16.

## ASSEMBLING THE QUILT TOP

1. Referring to the diagram below, arrange the blocks in four horizontal rows of four blocks each.

2. Sew the blocks into rows. Press the seams in alternate directions from row to row. Stitch the rows together. Press the seams in one direction.

3. Sew the blue stripe 1½" x 42" strips together end to end. Press seams open. Measure the length of the quilt through the center. From the pieced strip, cut two strips to this size. Sew one strip to each side of the quilt. Press seams toward the border.

4. Measure the width of the quilt through the center, including the side borders. Use the remaining pieced strip to cut two strips to this size and sew to the top and bottom of the quilt; press.

5. Measure the quilt as described in steps 3 and 4 to cut and sew outer-border strips using the red-and-blue 6" x 68" strips; press. Because these strips are cut on the lengthwise grain, they do not need to be pieced together.

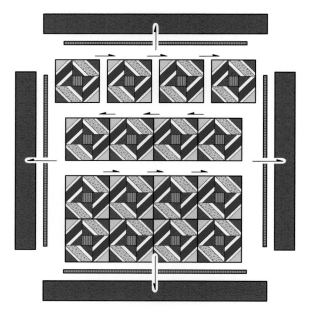

Assembly diagram

# FINISHING THE QUILT

1. Layer the quilt with batting and the pieced backing; baste. Hand or machine quilt as desired or refer to the quilting diagram that shows how the sample quilt was quilted.

2. Trim the batting and backing so the edges are even with the quilt top. Use the blue stripe 2" x 42" strips to bind the quilt.

**QUILTING SUGGESTION**

# JUNGLE STARS

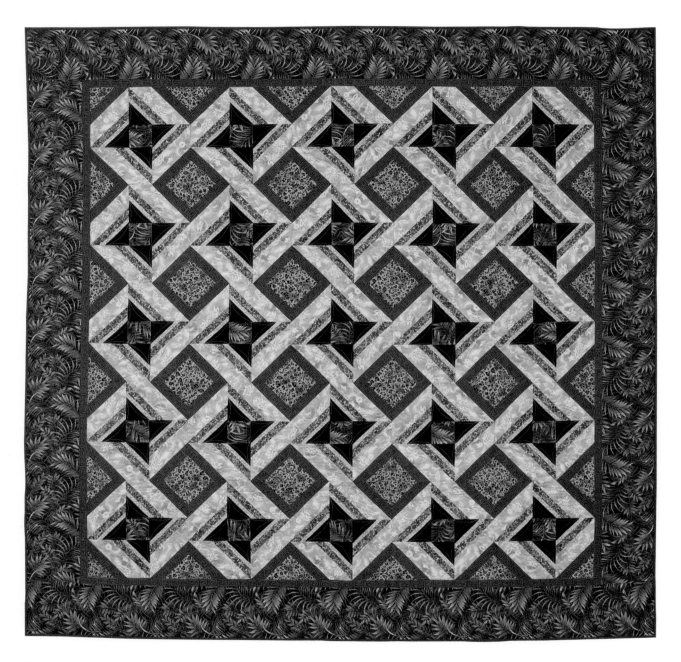

*I* love the rich, warm, earthy colors in this stunning quilt. It uses six-strip blocks that require a

little more time and patience but are well worth the effort.

**Finished Quilt Size:** 81½" x 81½"
**Finished Block Size:** 13" x 13"

## MATERIALS

*Yardage is based on 42"-wide fabric.*

5 yards of rust-with-spots print for blocks

3⅞ yards of beige floral print for blocks

3⅛ yards of medium brown print for blocks, inner border, and binding

2⅞ yards of dark brown tonal print for blocks

2⅝ yards of brown fern print for block centers and outer border

1⅔ yards of light brown print for blocks

1⅔ yards of tan print for blocks

8 yards of fabric for backing

86" x 86" piece of batting

| CUTTING | | | | |
|---|---|---|---|---|
| **Fabric** | **Use** | **Number to Cut** | **Size to Cut** | **Bias Strips*** |
| Dark brown print | Blocks | 5 pieces | 18" x 42" | 17 strips, 3¼" wide |
| Tan print | Blocks | 3 pieces | 18" x 42" | 34 strips, 1" wide |
| Light brown print | Blocks | 3 pieces | 18" x 42" | 34 strips, 1⅜" wide |
| Beige floral print | Blocks | 7 pieces | 18" x 42" | 34 strips, 2⅝" wide |
| Medium brown print | Blocks | 4 pieces | 18" x 42" | 34 strips, 1¾" wide |
| Medium brown print | Inner border | 7 strips | 1½" x 42" | — |
| Medium brown print | Binding | 9 strips | 2" x 42" | — |
| Rust-with-spots print | Blocks | 9 pieces | 18" x 42" | 34 strips, 3¼" wide |
| Brown fern print | Outer border | 4 lengthwise strips | 7½" x 84" | — |
| Brown fern print | Block centers | 25 squares | 3½" x 3½" | — |
| *\*Refer to "Cutting Bias Strips" on page 7 for detailed instructions if needed.* | | | | |

## Making the Blocks

1. Refer to "Making Strip Sets and Block Units" on page 7 to arrange and sew the strips together as shown. Press the seam allowances in one direction. Make 17 strip sets. Cut *each* strip set into six 5½" x 8½" rectangle units for a total of 102 units. You will have two extra rectangles.

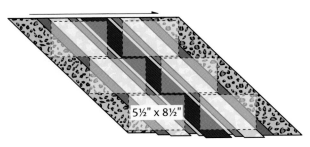

5½" x 8½"

Make 17 strip sets.
Cut 6 units from each strip set (102 total).

2. For ease in sewing the units together, arrange four rectangle units as shown. The top-right and bottom-left units will have the seam allowances pressed toward the outside edges. The top-left and bottom-right units will have the seam allowances pressed toward the center. Refer to "Assembling the Blocks" on page 9 to sew the units and a brown 3½" square together using the partial seam technique. Make 25 blocks.

Make 25.

## Assembling the Quilt Top

1. Refer to the diagram below to arrange the blocks into five horizontal rows of five blocks each.

2. Sew the blocks into rows. Press the seams in alternate directions from row to row. Stitch the rows together. Press the seams in one direction.

3. Sew the brown 1½" x 42" strips together end to end. Press seams open. Measure the length of the quilt through the center. From the pieced strip, cut two strips to this size. Sew one strip to each side of the quilt. Press seams toward the border.

4. Measure the width of the quilt through the center, including the side borders. Use the remaining pieced strip to cut two strips to this size and sew to the top and bottom of the quilt; press.

5. Measure the quilt as described in steps 3 and 4 to cut and sew outer-border strips using the brown 7½" x 84" strips; press. Because these strips are cut on the lengthwise grain, they do not need to be pieced together.

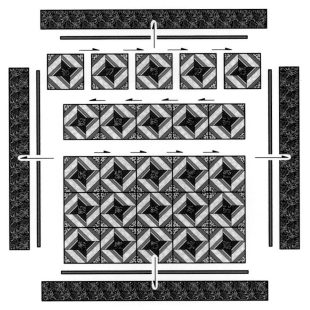

Assembly diagram

# Finishing the Quilt

1. Layer the quilt with batting and the pieced backing; baste. Hand or machine quilt as desired or refer to the quilting diagram that shows how the sample quilt was quilted.

2. Trim the batting and backing so the edges are even with the quilt top. Use the brown 2" x 42" strips to bind the quilt.

**QUILTING SUGGESTION**

# ABOUT THE AUTHOR

Author, teacher, fabric designer, and award-winning quiltmaker Nancy Mahoney has enjoyed making quilts for more than 20 years. An impressive range of her beautiful quilts has been featured in many national and international quilt magazines.

*Ribbon Star Quilts* is Nancy's eighth book with Martingale & Company. Her other bestselling books include *Square Deal* (2007) and *Quilt Revival* (2006).

Almost entirely self-taught, Nancy continues to explore new ways to combine traditional blocks and create quilts that are fun and easy to make.

Nancy lives in Florida with her life partner of more than 30 years, Tom, and their umbrella cockatoo, Prince.

# NEW AND BESTSELLING TITLES FROM

## APPLIQUÉ
Adoration Quilts
Appliqué at Play
**Cutting-Garden Quilts—***NEW!*
Favorite Quilts from Anka's Treasures
Mimi Dietrich's Baltimore Basics
**Mimi Dietrich's Favorite Appliqué Quilts—***NEW!*
Sunbonnet Sue and Scottie Too
Tea in the Garden

## FOCUS ON WOOL
The Americana Collection
Needle Felting
**Needle-Felting Magic—***NEW!*
Simply Primitive

## GENERAL QUILTMAKING
All Buttoned Up
**Bits and Pieces—***NEW!*
Bound for Glory
Calendar Kids
**Charmed—***NEW!*
Christmas with Artful Offerings
Colorful Quilts
Comfort and Joy
**Cool Girls Quilt—***NEW!*
Creating Your Perfect Quilting Space
A Dozen Roses
Fig Tree Quilts
Follow-the-Line Quilting Designs
Follow-the-Line Quilting Designs
    Volume Two
A Fresh Look at Seasonal Quilts
**The Little Box of Quilter's Chocolate
    Desserts—***NEW!*
Modern Primitive Quilts
Points of View
Positively Postcards
Prairie Children and Their Quilts
Quilt Revival
Quilter's Block-a-Day Calendar
Quilting in the Country

Sensational Sashiko
**Simple Seasons—***NEW!*
**Simple Seasons Recipe Cards—***NEW!*
Simple Traditions
Twice Quilted
Young at Heart Quilts

## LEARNING TO QUILT
Color for the Terrified Quilter
Happy Endings, Revised Edition
Let's Quilt!
Your First Quilt Book (or it should be!)

## PAPER PIECING
300 Paper-Pieced Quilt Blocks
Easy Machine Paper Piecing
Paper-Pieced Mini Quilts
Show Me How to Paper Piece
Showstopping Quilts to Foundation Piece
Spellbinding Quilts

## PIECING
40 Fabulous Quick-Cut Quilts
Better by the Dozen
Big 'n Easy
Clever Quarters, Too
**Mosaic Picture Quilts—***NEW!*
New Cuts for New Quilts
**Nine by Nine—***NEW!*
**Sew Fun, Sew Colorful Quilts—***NEW!*
Sew One and You're Done
Snowball Quilts
Square Deal
Sudoku Quilts
Twosey-Foursey Quilts
Wheel of Mystery Quilts

## QUILTS FOR BABIES & CHILDREN
Even More Quilts for Baby
Lickety-Split Quilts for Little Ones
The Little Box of Baby Quilts
Quilts for Baby
Sweet and Simple Baby Quilts

## SCRAP QUILTS
Nickel Quilts
Save the Scraps
Simple Strategies for Scrap Quilts

## CRAFTS
101 Sparkling Necklaces
**Art from the Heart—***NEW!*
**The Beader's Handbook—***NEW!*
Card Design
Creative Embellishments
**Crochet for Beaders—***NEW!*
It's a Wrap
It's in the Details
The Little Box of Beaded Bracelets
    and Earrings
The Little Box of Beaded Necklaces
    and Earrings
Miniature Punchneedle Embroidery
A Passion for Punchneedle
Punchneedle Fun
Scrapbooking off the Page…
    and on the Wall
Sculpted Threads
**Sew Sentimental—***NEW!*

## KNITTING & CROCHET
**365 Crochet Stitches a Year:
    Perpetual Calendar—***NEW!*
365 Knitting Stitches a Year:
    Perpetual Calendar
A to Z of Knitting
Crocheted Pursenalities
First Crochet
First Knits
Fun and Funky Crochet
**Handknit Skirts—***NEW!*
Handknit Style II
The Knitter's Book of Finishing
    Techniques
Knitting Circles around Socks
Knitting with Gigi
The Little Box of Crocheted Throws
The Little Box of Knitted Throws
Modern Classics
More Sensational Knitted Socks
Pursenalities
Top Down Sweaters
Wrapped in Comfort

Our books are available at bookstores and your favorite craft,
fabric, and yarn retailers. If you don't see the title you're looking for,
visit us at **www.martingale-pub.com** or contact us at:

## 1-800-426-3126

**International:** 1-425-483-3313 • **Fax:** 1-425-486-7596 • **Email:** info@martingale-pub.com